THE LITTLE BOOK OF MARMITE TIPS

THE LITTLE BOOK OF MARMITE TIPS

PAUL HARTLEY

Absolute Press

First published in Great Britain in 2007 by
Absolute Press, an imprint of Bloomsbury Publishing Plc
Scarborough House, 29 James Street West
Bath BA1 2BT, England
Phone +44 (0)1225 316013 **Fax** +44 (0)1225 445836
E-mail office@absolutepress.co.uk
Web www.absolutepress.co.uk

Reprinted 2008, 2009, 2010 (twice), 2011, 2012, 2013, 2014.

A catalogue record of this book is available from the British Library

ISBN 13: 9781904573777

Printed and bound by Hung Hing, China

Bloomsbury Publishing Plc
50 Bedford Square, London WC1B 3DP | www.bloomsbury.com
Bloomsbury is a trademark of Bloomsbury Publishing Plc.

Love it. Hate it.

Marmite

A touch of Marmite added to bread can make

great croutons for soup.

Spread it thinly onto the bread and then cut into cubes. Either toast under the grill or drizzle with olive oil and roast in the oven.

Create **the best burgers for kids.** Spread the baps with a little Marmite before adding the beefburger, onion and salad. It makes a delicious and balanced meal.

If your partner

loves kissing but hates Marmite,

keep a pack cf peppermints in the cupboard next to the Marmite jar, for instart mouth freshening.

To make a gorgeous savoury glaze for

heavenly
veggie pies,

mix a little Marmite with boiling water and brush over the uncooked pastry.

For a savoury crumb coating

on meat and vegetables, spread over a thin coat of Marmite and then dip into breadcrumbs. Chill before cooking.

Warm the knife or spoon

before application to ensure that your Marmite is delivered in its entirety to the chosen destination.

Two teaspoons of Marmite to one pint of

water makes **a quick**

and easy stock

for any savoury dish.

Adding Marmite to a **cheese sauce** reduces the amount of cheese required to give a **good strong flavour.** Stir it into the hot sauce just before serving or baking your gratin.

A Marmite Mum

can get all the Folic acid she needs in her diet from four slices of bread and Marmite a day.

Enhance the flavour of the filling in your savoury pancakes

by adding Marmite to the batter. Use half a teaspoon for a batter that serves four to six people.

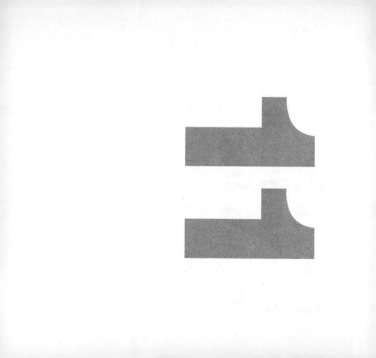

Empty Jar Uses No. 1:

A clean, empty Marmite pot makes the perfect herb or spice jar. The shape is ideal to display on your shelf and the **dark glass will keep your dried herbs in good condition.**

Fresh **watercress and Marmite are a marriage made in heaven.**

Toast two slices of your favourite bread, then spread with butter and Marmite. Lay on some watercress and sandwich together. Cut into strips and you'll have perfectly seasoned soldiers for dipping into your boiled egg (salt from the Marmite and pepper from the watercress).

Don't throw away spent

Marmite
Squeezy pots.

Wash them out and fill them from the tap – they

make great
water pistols.

Wrap up your Marmite.

Mix half a teaspoon of Marmite with two tablespoons of mayo and spread a thin layer over a soft flour tortilla. Lay some sliced, ccoked chicken breast and sliced avocado across t1e centre, wrap up and devour.

Mix three teaspoons of Marmite with one tablespoon of hot water in a roasting pan to

coat chipolatas

baked in the oven. When Marmite is cooked it decreases in strength so you will end up with a really enhanced meaty sausage that are not overpowered by the Marmite.

Rescuing the Dregs No.1:

When you can't get one more scraping out of your Marmite jar, simply pour in hot water, stir and use for gravy.

For a little **extra zing in your Eggs Florentine** stir a teaspoon of Marmite into the Hollandaise sauce before pouring it over the egg, spinach and muffin.

Mashed bananas and Marmite

on toasted brown bread soldiers make a great teatime treat for kids whilst they do their homework. Most kids love the mixed flavours of sweet and savoury.

To create an amazing crust to a roast rib of beef,

blend together English mustard and Marmite and slather it over the meat.

Like old honey, **dryish**

Marmite can be reconstituted

by submerging the jar in simmering water for a few minutes. Marmite can be stored at room temperature, even after opening. Large jars will last months – even years – without spoiling.

Adding Marmite when making short-crust pastry results in a

savoury crust
for pies, quiches and pasties.

Add **Marmite** to your **vinaigrette** and drizzle over a salad of crispy lettuce, sliced boiled egg and new potatos. The addition of a little saltiness to the vinaigrette combo **makes** this **salad irresistible.**

Use Marmite as a mosquito repellent when travelling in hot countries.

Whilst there isn't a scientific proof to confirm that it works, many experienced travellers have it for breakfast, lunch or tea and will not travel without it.

24

Thick tcast with lots of Marmite will aid

recovery from a hangover.

It's the vitamin B that helps soothe the stomach and calm the blood that's causing the headache.

Letting the kids create pictures on their toast with

Marmite
Squeezy

provides them with a good breakfast and

encourages
artistic flair.

For fantastic roasted root vegetables

add a little Marmite to warm sunflower oil and brush over half way through their cooking. It will bring them to life, lift the flavour and finish them with a crispy glaze.

To make

savoury rusks, perfect for Marmite toddlers,

cut slices of bread into fingers, spread thinly with Marmite and cook in a very low oven for a couple of hours.

Stirring a teaspoon of **Marmite** into **devilled kidneys** just before serving will bring out the flavour of the kidneys. They will **taste great** served on toasted triangles with a flourish of fresh parsley.

Rescuing the Dregs No.2:

To get every last bit of goodness from your Marmite jar, add a little boiling water to the near-empty pot and stir around. Tip out into a cup, add some cooler water and enjoy

a really satisfying savoury drink.

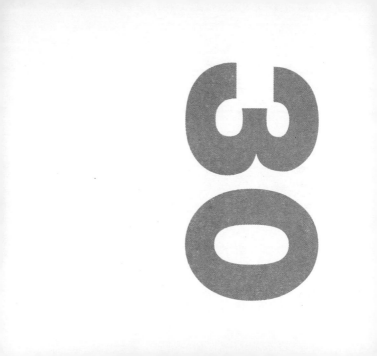

Stir Marmite **into** warm **baked beans** add chunks of crispy bacon and pile on sourdough toast really fulfilling brunch and a **flavour of the Wild West.**

Add a teaspoon of Marmite to your mix when you **make Yorkshire puddings.**

It will make them **crispier** when cooked.

Marmite fun for all the family.

Toast some baked square slices of bread, then butter and spread with Marmite and trim off the crusts. Cut each slice into nine equal squares and present them on a flat plate for the children – and adults! – to build a train, a car... whatever you can think of. Form extra shapes with cookie cutters. It will help stimulate your children at mealtimes.

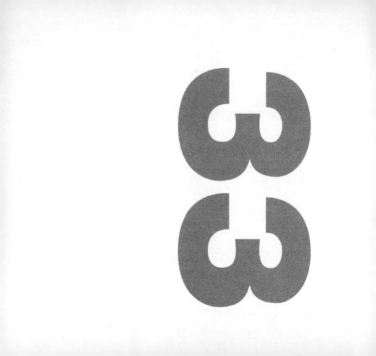

A hearty broth

made from Marmite makes the perfect base

for noodle soup **on a cold**

winter's day.

For a tasty coating for roast leg of lamb,

mix a teaspoon of Marmite, a teaspoon of honey and a teaspoon of wholegrain mustard with chopped fresh herbs and spread over the meat before placing in the oven.

Leticia's worst Marmite tip.

DO NOT ice your cake with a mixture of Marmite and 'tasamaralata' unless you want to make *The Vicar of Dibley* sick.

For double-scrummy garlic bread

mix a little Marmite with unsalted butter and finely chopped garlic and spread onto a sliced baguette (with some on the crust as well). Wrap in foil and bake for 20 minutes, unwrapping the foil for the last few minutes to crispen up the crust.

Minced beef sometimes lacks a little flavour, so add a teaspoon of **Marmite** to **your Spaghetti Bolognese** sauce 10 minutes before the end of cooking time.

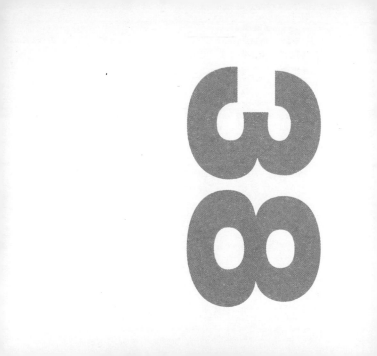

Always save limited edition Marmite

There are millions of Marmiteenies

jars. out there as these **may well**

become valuable **collectors'**

items.

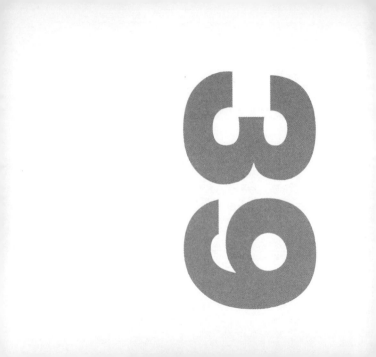

Spread a little Marmite onto **sweet potato wedges** and sprinkle over some fresh thyme leaves before roasting them in a hot oven. When golden and crispy, serve with sour cream or yoghurt – it will **make a veggie heaven starter.**

When introducing young children to Marmite soldiers make sure you **spread it very thinly** at first. Any thicker a layer will be too much of an assault on their inquisitive taste bucs.

For a quick and easy **Marmite party snack,** roll out some readymade puff pastry into a large rectangle, spread with Marmite and sprinkle with grated cheese. Roll up the pastry and cut thin slices **like Catherine wheels.** Bake in a hot oven for 20 minutes.

Empty Jar Uses No.2:

Drop lit nightlights into a row of empty 250g Marmite jars and line them down the centre of your table

for stylish alfresco dining.

For a supremely balanced breakfast

spread hot buttered toast with Marmite and then pile scrambled eggs on top. Serve with a glass of freshly squeezed orange juice and Voila! – a full complement of vitamins A, B, C, D & E!

Crudités and breadsticks need a tasty companion

so mix together some cream cheese, Marmite, chopped coriander and a dash of chilli sauce and you will have a Marmite Island Dip.

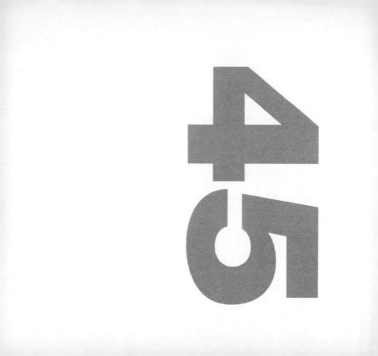

Stir-fry magic.

reach for

When you the soy sauce and find you've run out try adding

a little **Marmite** to the wok –

you'll be amazed how good your stir-fry tastes.

An empty Marmite Squeezy pot is

the fun way
to take your
factor 15
to the beach

this summer. Watch the disbelief on the faces of your friends' as they watch you oiling up!

Adding Marmite and chopped watercress to **mashed potato** really lifts the flavour – but have fun adding the Marmite by playing **noughts and crosses** with your Squeezy on a plateau of the mash first!

Mix Marmite with textured vegetable protein (TVP) to

pamper your pooch

with a healthy alternative to meat-based dog food.

Rescuing the Dregs No.3:

Add hot water to the last bit in the Marmite jar and stir. Then, when boiling or steaming vegetables you can add it to the water which will save you having to add salt.

For an easily

portable pot
of vinaigrette,

take your empty Marmite Squeezy pot, fill it with
dressing and then stash into your work lunchbox
or picnic hamper. Prior to use, give it a good
shake to ensure that the flavours are well mixed
and then dress your salad.

Paul Hartley

Paul Hartley is the bestselling author of *The Marmite Cookbook* (Absolute Press) and a truly dedicated evangelist for the culinary wonders of Marmite. His innovative powers with this iconic storecupboard spread know no bounds – his fantastic Fudges™ Marmite Biscuits and these fifty tips prevail as testimony. He is also the author of *The Lea & Perrins Cookbook, The Colman's Mustard Cookbook, The Heinz Tomato Ketchup Cookbook* and *The Lyle's Golden Syrup Cookbook*. A gifted food writer, but also a talented chef who has in past lives run European-style café-bars in London and an award-winning country pub in Somerset. He is a major contributor to www.breakfastandbrunch.com.

ANDREW LANGLEY
THE LITTLE BOOK OF
SPICE TIPS

THE LITTLE BOOK OF
POKER TIPS

ANDREW LANGLEY
THE LITTLE BOOK OF
BARBECUE TIPS

PETER FRENCH
THE LITTLE BOOK OF
GOLF TIPS

WILLIAM FORTT
THE LITTLE BOOK OF
GARDENING TIPS

ANDREW LANGLEY
THE LITTLE BOOK OF
BEER TIPS

THE LITTLE BOOK OF
TIPS SERIES

RICHARD FROGGS
THE LITTLE BOOK OF
CHEFS' TIPS

WILLIAM FORTT
THE LITTLE BOOK OF
HERB TIPS

THE LITTLE BOOK OF **AGA TIPS**²
RICHARD MAGGS

THE LITTLE BOOK OF **AGA TIPS**³
RICHARD MAGGS

THE LITTLE BOOK OF **RAYBURN TIPS**
RICHARD MAGGS

THE LITTLE BOOK OF **WINE TIPS**
ANDREW LANGLEY

THE LITTLE BOOK OF **TEA TIPS**
ANDREW LANGLEY

THE LITTLE BOOK OF **CHRISTMAS AGA TIPS**
RICHARD MAGGS

THE LITTLE BOOK OF **CHEESE TIPS**
ANDREW LANGLEY

THE LITTLE BOOK OF **COFFEE TIPS**
ANDREW LANGLEY

THE LITTLE BOOK OF **AGA TIPS**
RICHARD MAGGS

THE LITTLE BOOK OF PUPPY TIPS
ANDREW LANGLEY

THE LITTLE BOOK OF GREEN TIPS
WILLIAM FORTT

THE LITTLE BOOK OF BRIDGE TIPS
PETER FRENCH

THE LITTLE BOOK OF WHISKY TIPS
ANDREW LANGLEY

THE LITTLE BOOK OF KITTEN TIPS
ANDREW LANGLEY

THE LITTLE BOOK OF CHESS TIPS
PETER FRENCH

THE LITTLE BOOK OF TRAVEL TIPS
MEGAN DEVENISH

THE LITTLE BOOK OF MARMITE TIPS
PAUL HARTLEY

THE LITTLE BOOK OF FISHING TIPS
NICK DEVENISH

Little Books of Tips
from Absolute Press

Aga Tips
Aga Tips 2
Aga Tips 3
Allotment Tips
Backgammon Tips
Barbecue Tips
Beer Tips
Bread Tips
Bread Machine Tips
Bridge Tips
Cake Baking Tips
Cake Decorating Tips
Champagne Tips
Cheese Tips
Chefs' Tips
Chess Tips
Chocolate Tips
Christmas Aga Tips

Chutney and Pickle Tips
Cocktail Tips
Coffee Tips
Cupcake Tips
Curry Tips
Fishing Tips
Fly Fishing Tips
Frugal Tips
Gardening Tips
Golf Tips
Green Tips
Grow Your Own Tips
Herb Tips
Houseplant Tips
Ice Cream Tips
Jam Tips
Kitten Tips
Macaroon Tips

Marmite Tips
Olive Oil Tips
Pasta Tips
Poker Tips
Puppy Tips
Rayburn Tips
Slow Cooker Tips
Spice Tips
Tea Tips
Travel Tips
Whisky Tips
Wine Tips
Wok Tips
Vinegar Tips